A Unique Collection of Poems

of

POEMS

AND PERSONAL EXPERIENCES

Dex McLaughlin

A UNIQUE COLLECTION OF POEMS AND PERSONAL EXPERIENCES

iUniverse books may be ordered through booksellers or by contacting:

iUniverse
1663 Liberty Drive
Bloomington, IN 47403
www.iuniverse.com
844-349-9409

ISBN: 978-1-6632-2580-1 (sc)
ISBN: 978-1-6632-2693-8 (e)

Library of Congress Control Number: 2021916585

Print information available on the last page.

iUniverse rev. date: 08/18/2021

DEDICATION

This book is dedicated to my lovely fiance Judy Trotz, thanks for being my ride or die, babe. Also to my son Joshua Douglas McLaughlin, life is short kid, make the most of it. And to the folks with an open mind and willing to read some fresh material from young aspiring writers like myself. And last but not least, to all who have been there for me, You know who you are. " Thank You!"

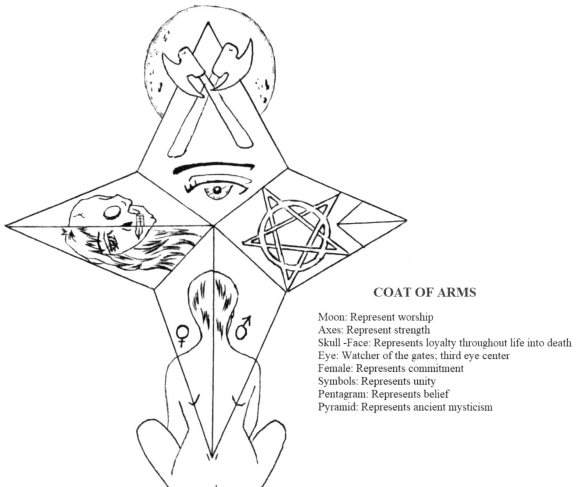

COAT OF ARMS

Moon: Represent worship
Axes: Represent strength
Skull -Face: Represents loyalty throughout life into death
Eye: Watcher of the gates; third eye center
Female: Represents commitment
Symbols: Represents unity
Pentagram: Represents belief
Pyramid: Represents ancient mysticism

"Sixty-Nine Me"

1 I rise up you swallow me down I was lost but now I'm found
2 I feel the magic underneath your dress I feel your wetness what a beautiful mess

1 Rising up to meet your lips I taste your sex as I drink it from your hips
2 Silk and satin leather and lace take off your panties and sit on my face

1 Everytime you caress my balls I let loose like Niagra Falls.
2 You feel my tounge in between your thighs you say you love me, your so full of lies.

1 I'm so hard - I'm so full of desire - kiss me baby let the fire burn higher
2 That's Ok - your oral sex is great, I love the way you fornicate

1 Call me baby - Call me soon - Find your way into my room and sixty-nine me
2 Fornicate - the way we should I want it baby and I want it good sixty-nine me

1 Sixty nine me - sixty nine me - all night long everytime I smell your scent
2 Sixty nine me bump and grind. All night long - you make me horny, with that look in your eye.

1 I rise up man - your heaven scent - heaven sent - your wings take me higher
2 You make me cum - when I'm deep in your thighs, sixty nine me - all night long.

1 Girl you light my soul on fire.
2 From the couch - Out to the lawn. Even though, it may be a crime - I'll munch again - That Eat-N's Prime yummy!

"Rusted Halo"

I loved the way we were when our love was standing strong.
Hard to believe we fell apart and that its been that long ago.

When I think about the days up at Willy's place. I get an empty feeling, oh oo how I miss your face

Really no need to feel all that sad, holding onto all these memories - Hoping I'll see you someday yes I hope - and I pray that I get a chance to say.

That I missed the way we danced underneath those neon lights. The way we kissed so passionately the way you held me on a moonlit night.
That night - I glimpsed your soul.

This love comes easy baby let me in. Falling in love all over again.
Don't ask why, no need to cry I love your sin I want your lust desire. Maybe you'll see me someday - and I'll pay - you'll want to stay

Bridge -
Spread your wings, lets hit the wind
Fly so high - out where the angels fly. Ain't no running from the keeper of the souls

Chorus:
When this lifes no more - The halo drops the angels cry. Spread your wings & hit the wind. Fly so high never to be seen again.
When this lifes no more - your halo drops the angels cry - the angels cry
Out beyond the deep blue sky - there's a place where the angels fly. Never wanna have to say goodbye.
But there ain't no running from the keeper of the souls.

RIDE THE WIND

Sometimes - we let go of - the things - more im-portant than the ones - we hold on - to -

What can I do? - I'm still in love with you in my heart - I truly miss you. I should have never have let you go -

The regrets - they are many - broken hearts - they never mend. And I'll probably never see you again.

But those memories - I'll hang on to cause the songs of yesterday they live I'm lost in one now.

Singin the blues bout the love I lost with you. A cowboys pride can't be kept in side - what might have been. I'll never know.

Chorus.
Ride the wind, yeah that's what I'll do - ride the wind
Playing our song - and thinking of you - ride the wind
No easy way to pretend ride the wind onto the bitter end.
I'm riding the wind. Lonesome is where I stand.
Yeah this is where it ends.

COLD SHOULDER

When I saw you yesterday - I told you I was home for good - that I was here to stay - you said, you never thought you would You gave me the cold shoulder - and walked away from me.

It brought me to my knees - you said that you would never leave - and now your giving me the cold shoulder - I can't live here on my own - its your love that makes this a home - whose to blame? -

Baby kiss me one more time - bring your lips close to mine.
Light some candles, crack open some wine - tell me everything will be just fine. I'm in love with you. It really brought me to my knees.

I'm begging baby, baby, please - don't give me the cold shoulder. I thought I knew what love is - I never knew it could feel like this. When I was with you it felt so right - now I toss and turn [cold and lonely]

Yes I'm out here on my own - all because of your heart of stone. And your cold shoulder that's okay baby its your loss. Nothing comes without its cost - look what we lost.

If you ever find yourself in need - just remember that my heart is free - from your cold shoulder. Were both playin a losing game, think I'll give you a taste of the same - of your cold shoulder
Cold shoulder x3 I'm giving you the cold shoulder.

"FUCK YOU"

Fuck you for what you said
Fuck the day we went to bed
Fuck the trip that you've been on.
Fuck the place your pussy's gone
Fuck you and the way you lied
And also fuck the reason why.
Fuck all the times I almost cried.
And fuck the bastard you tried to hide
I'll make you wish you fucking died.
I'll put a hole in that fucked up pride.
Fuck the car and fuck the truck
Fuck you and you fucked up luck
Fuck your pissy & whiney moods
You need to take some fucking ludes.
Fuck the cat and fuck the dog.
You probably fucked the farmers hog.
So fucking pack and fucking go
I'm so tired of this fucking show
Fuck the sink and fuck the drain
Fuck you and your fucked up brain
Fuck you and your phony tears
I've wasted all these fucking years.
You fucking cunt you fucking bitch.
I should've left you in a fucking ditch
Fuck the beginning and fuck the end.
Fuck you and your fucked up friends
Fuck the smoke and fuck the gas
Fuck you and your big fat ass.
Fuck the middle and fuck the rest
You ain't even the fucking best.

Fuck you cunt!

These are personal opinions and experiences that I thought would fit well with the book.

Feb 2 2021

Dex McLaughlin

Dexter McLaughlin
9-25-12
Education

I believe I can change my self-will run ride behavior by cultivating my spirit through spiritual practice, keyword being practice, because until I change my inner-being I will more than likely keep doing the same things. My first realization is knowing the difference between religion, and spirituality. Being religious connotes belonging to and practicing a religious tradition, being spiritual suggests a personal commitment to a process of inner development that engages me in my totality, so, when "authentic" faith embodies my spirituality, only then will religious and spiritual coincide. Deep down I know that spirituality has to become a way of life that affects and includes every moment of my existence. To be spiritual I must stand on my own two feet while "being" nurtured and supported by my tradition. However, I must not depend on an institution, my church, whatever, or whoever to make my decisions, I must look for "inner" direction. I must shape my spiritual life through conformity to external piety. I must not lose the ability and desire to stand on my own two feet. My spirituality must draw me into the depths of my being where I can come face to face with myself, my weaknesses, and with ultimate mystery. I understand that life is a spiritual journey, and that I must take this journey alone, even while surrounded by loved ones, and how I make this journey is what spirituality is all about, finding my own path is part of what it means to have a measure of independence and inner directedness. This evolution of my individual spirituality is a mysterious and intimate matter and originates in my heart, it is a deep stirring that represents an insatiable longing for fulfillment. There are many ways that I can begin to live a day-to-day spiritual reality, I can have a sacramental vision of the natural world around me, for nature is full of lessons. I can have a direct awareness of the divine in the immanence of nature, in other beings, and in my own community existence.

The older I get the more I see and realize that children and younger people are naturally spiritual because they have a need, a passion for meaning, kind of like a passion for the infinite. There is alot to be learned from children, but I must open my eyes and "see". I have to embrace my spiritual journey, I can't concern myself to what others are doing, I must find my own way, and must be faithful to the truth I know or discover. I tend to look at all the traditions of the spiritual life and kind of adopt an attitude of inter-spirituality, I claim the wisdom dimension of all traditions for myself and I let that wisdom guide me, if I find others approach to this subject troubled, I don't reject it, I build on it. If I gain perspective on the influences of the culture and people in my life, it will allow my inner values, voice, and vision to emerge into clarity. In sum, I must not give into the temptation of cynicism and despair, for cynicism and despair our diseases of the spirit, they reduce my inner freedom and plunges me into moral, intellectual, and spiritual inertia, they will freeze my development and any hope of discovering ultimate meaning, direction, and belonging in life I must cast off skepticism and be a radiant presence of depth, love, and kindness to others. I must cultivate a love of quietness, learn to appreciate it, avoid noise, confusion, chaos, and needless tension. I believe that the stillness, quiet, or silence is the divine presence itself, that its a summons, an invitation into ultimate realization. And as I become more proficient with the stillness, I should let my spiritual practice revolve around that stillness by adopting some form of meditation practice, and I believe this will help transform me. And last but not least, I must dare to be different, dare to be myself, be who I really am. Be who I know myself to be in my moments of greatest clarity. I must not let others determine my identity for me, and not give away my power of self-determination.

500 W/E On How My Next ID Could Be A Toe Tag.

Dexter McLaughlin
9-25-12
Education

Commitment

This is my five hundred word essay on how my next I.D. could be my toe tag. For this essay I really had to take a look at my life past, present, and future. I am on my fourth state number. I look back and now realize that this prisons shit isn't for me. I need to make a whole lot of changes in my life so my next I.D. is not my toe tag. There is many things that could happen that could lead to my next I.D. being my toe tag. Like if I was to take this therapeutic community as joke and not learn shit I could go home and drink and use drugs. I could keep drinking everyday and end up abusing my liver so much that it could fail or get cirrhosis of the liver. I could go out drinking with some buddies get drunk and think I am able to drive my friends and I home. I could cause an accident and kill my friends, myself and possibly an innocent bystander. I could get out and need money so I think it will be OK to just sell drugs for some fast money. In the process of me selling drugs I could be robbed and maybe killed or kill someone else then I could end up in prison for the rest of my life or get end up six feet under because I made a very bad decision. If I do not take recovery serious I could go home and start using drugs and alcohol. I could get a bad batch of drugs or even to pure and end up overdosing. If I get to bad into my addiction I could go into someones home and they could wake up while I'm there and kill me. As you can see there is a whole lot of ways my next I.D. could be my toe tag. If I was to go home or act like a complete idiot and not use what I have learned this time in prison. I could get yet another state number and end up in a lot harder prison. While in there I could get into some shit like gambling or just owe someone something and maybe that person could beat me to death or even stab me with a homemade shank. There is many ways my addiction could lead me back to prison for the rest of my life which to me is just as bad as being in a morgue dead with a toe tag identifying me. Or I could just end up dead by overdose, disease, or murdered. Writing this essay made me realize I do not want that life anymore. I need to reevaluate my life and take in everything I can from the programs the state put on my prescriptive plan. I don't want to end up dead because of something I could have avoided by applying what I've learned to my life. Thank you for giving me this essay. It has really made me think about the reality of my addiction.

Commitment: 500 W/E on Why Do I Think I'm So Special to Be Able to Use Women.

Dexter McLaughlin
Education
9-27-12

I had to put alot of thought into this question, and came to the conclusion that even though I manipulated women, I still am special, as we all are, including the women I've used or hurt in the past. Its a matter of incorrect thinking and narcissistic behaviour, and stuns from numerous factors, such as upbringing, learned behaviors, and all other manner of influences. She used me to feel better about herself. I believe this may have been the starting point, or one of the influencing factors to believing it was OK to just use women, for it seems that after this incident, I lost all emotional attachment towards women and felt that I wasn't going to let this happen to me again. I started to feel that they are for me and my needs and that is it. I started seeking at insecure women because I knew that they were (and still are) easily manipulated, I knew all they really wanted was for someone to love them, so I preyed on this and in return they would fulfill my every need & desire. I saw how far a simple compliment could take me. And when I saw that they were more than willing to provide me with a roof over my head, supply me in drugs and alcohol, drive me everywhere I needed to go and give me great sex, I became totally complacent with this lifestyle, I wasn't keeping it real, back then it was all about the partying, sex, and the thrill of the "catch", when one fling died out, I found that my looks and charisma carried me easily over to the next woman, who again, was more than willing to oblige me in my indulgences, even after I developed a reputation for being a user! I couldn't figure that one out, but believe me, I ran with it, more food for the ego! So I basically became a spoiled little brat. I should also mention that I was raised by women, no father figure, was always babied, because to my mom, and my my grandma, I am special, and this feeling of special that I felt cultivated into a false reality on what my place in a relationship should actually be. My addiction being the number one factor in impeding productive, positive growth mentally & emotionally, which kind of manifested itself into an over-inflated ego. However, today, I do not take on this shallow view of women, wisdom comes with age, and believe it or not, I have learned so much from my past mistakes. In hindsight, its not that I truly set out to hurt a women, I was ignorant to the fact that those were real emotion I was playing with, I was misguided & misdirected, I really had no positive influences, I pretty much learned everything the hard way, after-all, experience is the best teacher! I feel much more content with who I am today as a person and have forgiven myself so that I can move on, and I truly believe that I have alot to offer some lucky woman someday due to the fact that I am remorseful of my past and choose to keep things real for this moment forward. Women are not just sex objects, they are human beings with feelings and emotions, in closing, I'll say that I love women and think they are an awesome compliment to the male species. I creator sure knew what he was doing!

Committment: 500 W/E on How I Plan to Stay Out of Prison;

Dexter McLaughlin
Education
9-15-12

Upon being released from prison I have alot of challenges ahead of me if I want to stay out of prison and better my life. My first thing I plan to accomplish is obtaining steady employment. This step alone I feel will benefit me in many ways. It will provide me with the money I need to sustain myself in life as well as a sense of fulfillment and accomplishment. This job will also give me less idol time in which to get myself into trouble. The next step in my plan to stay out of prison is to attend regular AA meetings and obtain AA sponsorship to further myself in the 12 step program and stay focused on my recovery. Interacting with the AA community will be a vital part of my staying out of prison and remaining sober, through the AA community and my sponsor I will always have someone to turn to when I'm down and feeling stressed. Along with getting involved in the AA community in my area I also plan to find other positive organizations to possibly volunteer my time. I also plan to work hard to improve my family relations by spending more time with my loved ones and giving them the attention they missed out on by me being in prison. I plan to attend family events and be a better family, as where in the past I may I have locked in some of these areas due to my behavior during my addiction and my incarceration. As I am working on the aforementioned goals I also plan to become more integrated into my community, where before, this really never mattered to me. I plan to attend community sanctioned events, as well as volunteer my help at these events. I also plan to pay more attention to and participate in the election of my communities officials to ensure my communities well-being in the future. I want to be proud of the community I live in and plan to put my own effort into it to help make it a better place for others as well. Beyond these responsibilities I will also need to make all of my parole appointments, I shall balance parole restrictions with my long-term goals. However, once off parole. I can focus all my attention on the goals here-in. The last part of my plan is to distance myself from negative people and places I used to hang around and spend (or waste) time with. Since my lifestyle is changing from negative to positive. I have no need to subject myself to the things these people lead me to any longer. Of course, this is a flexible, working plan, in the event something should arise out of left field.

Commitment: 500 W/E on King Baby Packet.

Dexter McLaughlin
9-15-12
Education

This is my five hundred word essay on the King Baby packet. King Baby is an infantile ego we have in our unconscious mind. The packet states that chemically dependent should especially be aware of the King Baby characteristics because these behaviors and attitudes can mess us up in our recovery. After reading over the King Baby packet I feel King Baby is us as people acting like infants. Like when we were babies and our parents gave us everything when we cried and whined. We grow up and still have these characteristics that we let come out when we want something. Dr. Harry Tiebout says that "when infantile traits continue into adulthood, the person is spoken of as immature. "King Babies can show characteristics like having difficulty accepting personal criticism and get angry and defensive when criticized. King Babies are self-rejecting or self-alienated. They live in the past and are fearful of what the future holds. If you are all about money and material things this could be King Baby characteristic. Another characteristic could be if you think rules and laws are not for ourselves, but for others. Inside a lot of addicted people is a scared, lonely, shamed boy or girl. That constantly compare themselves to others and feel like they don't measure up. Feelings of worthlessness, self-blame, and I-don't belong become a major part of our personalities. King Baby comes out as a reaction to those feelings of shame and inadequacy. When we try to be accepted and to please others we begin to find things on the outside to make people like us feel better inside. Things like fast cars, expensive clothes, drugs, attractive lovers, and the excitement of fast living help soothe our pain. There is no amount of love, money, or fame that will satisfy the scared little boy inside of us. When seeing this as a weakness the King Baby in us will try to destroy, attack and push the scared little boy inside to the side. King Baby will help us block out the fact that the scared little boy inside us exists. There are two motivating factors that can help us understand King Baby. The first factor is the scared, lonely, child who does not want to be hurt anymore and the second factor is the King Baby is never satisfied. For us to have long-term recovery we need to regain self-worth and learn to control our King Baby behaviors. Power, attention, and pleasure are three big motives to our King Baby mentality. Alot of us fear being rejected as ourselves so we present a false, made-up person to the world. Which by doing this protects us from being hurt. King Babies can't stand it when things are going good so they will rock the boat or create a problem. By us surrendering to the twelve steps can harness the power of King Baby and can help us find a higher power that will work for us. In the program we can learn the true meaning of forgiveness, humility, and gratitude. We can learn to avoid the downfalls of King Baby by tuning into the twelve steps. We need to take responsibility for our own self worth and dignity. We need to get our personal power back by admitting our powerlessness over others. I feel that it will be a relief that I will no longer feel I gotta control everything. I'll let my higher power handle that.

Commitment: Long term After-Care and Support Groups

Dexter McLaughlin
???
(TXA.)
9-15-12
Education

This is my five hundred word essay on my long term aftercare, meetings I can attend and positive support groups. Well before long term aftercare I'll have to make realistic short term goals to work to a long term aftercare plan. For the short term I will complete this therapeutic community program. I will take in everything I have learned and will learn in this program so I have a solid foundation for when I do get released. Then when I am released I need to find a steady job, find a home group in either Alcoholics or Narcotics Anonymous start talking to men in the program and find a temporary sponsor until I find a permanent sponsor who is trustworthy and one I feel comfortable confiding in. Then I can start working on my long term aftercare. For starters I'll have to know my triggers that trigger me to use drugs and alcohol. Get settled into a home group in Alcoholics Anonymous or Narcotics Anonymous whichever one I feel the most comfortable going to. While I find my permanent sponsor which I'll be able to work the steps with. I know that I have to give everything I got into working the steps. People who honestly work the steps of either Alcoholics or Narcotics Anonymous are far more successful than people who work the program half-fast. The ultimate long term goal for me is to be drug and alcohol free and not have to worry about "coming back to prison. While working a steady job and providing for me and my family. There are many different meetings I can attend to help me in this recovery process. I can attend Alcoholics Anonymous when you all know is for people dependent on alcohol. I could go to Narcotics Anonymous which is for individuals dependent on drugs. For me I am not sure which one of these I will attend because I drink alcohol and use drugs. I know there's other meetings like S.O.S. but I feel I'll have better success in either NA or AA. Now for support groups that I can use to help me in my recovery. My Narcotics or Alcoholics anonymous sponsor and sober men in the program can be a good positive support group. A priest or pastor can be a positive support group. My mental health counselor can also be in my support group. If I decide to do an outpatient drug and alcohol program my counselor could be someone I can ask for help in my support group. Family and friend who have my best interest at heart is a very good as positive support group. As long as I can stay away from my old friends who I used to use with and places I use to go that triggered me to use. I need to stay away from the things that used to also trigger me to have that thought to use. I know if I have my positive support groups and use them affectively I will be able to overcome these obstacles. These are all things I need to follow to stay clean and sober. Go to my Narcotics and Alcoholics Anonymous meetings, work the steps with my sponsor, and keep in contact with my support groups. All these things will make my long-term aftercare work for me.

This is my "True" out of Body Experience first one I ever had.

Feb 2 2021

10-26-19

???

One night back in 2018, the exact date I do not recall, my fiancé and I were out doing a little drinking, and, in hindsight, we both clearly had to much to drink. I most certainly should not have been behind the wheel! As alcohol severely impairs ones ability for "good sense" & judgement. (To say the least)

Eventually an arguement ensues between her and I (another, among many negatives about alcohol!), and to this day, I cannot tell you what possessed me to speed up to 60 m.p.h., or more rounding a sharp incline turn where I encountered a pick-up truck coming right at me as I was in the wrong lane, in my haste, I abruptly swerved to the left which put us facing the other direction hitting the curb which sent us rolling over three or four times. Thankfully, no one but myself was injured as a result of my irresponsible behaviours and poor decisions that night!

When I opened my eyes there was a helicopter pilot informing me that I was in a bad car accident and, that my fiancé and I were being air lifted to U.P.M.C. Altoona, PA. Thankfully, she was not badly injured! Just a mildly bruised arm. I, on the other hand, received a cracked neck and vertebrae in my back. However, this story is not about my injuries I simply wanted to briefly explain the circumstances and events leading up to my out of body experience, which proceeds as follows: I awoke in the hospital at one time, long enough to say hi to my family and briefly speak with my fiancé whom explained to me again what had happened and said that the doctor wanted to keep me for a few days not to worry that she was staying with me at the hospital in the visitors lounge.

When I awoke again, I was hovering above my fiancé sleeping on an L shaped couch under flourescent lights near some vending machines, she was laying in a fetal position with a coat or something draped over her arms, then, one of the nurses, (whom I remembered seeing in my room), opened up a door and stepped in - all of a sudden, just like the flick of a light switch, I was back in my room fully awake thinking about what I had just seen and experienced? Strangely, it did not feel like a dream? I actually felt that I was in fact, in that room looking down at my fiancé!

Later that day, when my fiancé came to my room for a visit, I decided to test my theory (feeling) to prove to myself and my fiancé that what I felt like happened, in fact truly did happen. First and foremost, I did not mention my experience to her before I started questioning her, as this would have defeated my purpose!

She could tell by the perplexed look on my face that I was about to ask her something. And I asked her if I had left my room since I arrived? She said. "No", and the nurse confirmed it as well. I continued questioning her and asked if she was sleeping on an L shaped couch near some vending machines under fluorescent lights? With something draped over her? She looked at me astonished and said, "yes, how on earth did you know that?" That's when I shared my experience of hovering above her watching her sleep and that when a nurse walked in I had vanished in a blink of an eye right back to my hospital bed. In this manner of investigating the truth of my experience, I validated and confirmed to myself and, to her, that what had happened, actually happened!

Out of body experiences are most certainly not unheard of. Does it happen often? Not likely (but then again, I'm only in one part of this huge earth & universe?) Does it in fact, happen? "Yes, I know it does." Like I said, this and other phenomena is not unheard of, its just that the majority of folks do not experience them and simply just don't believe in other wordly things....I, on the other hand, have experienced some intense phenomena that just isn't to be ignored. Whether you believe in such matters, or, occult philosophy in general, makes no difference either way in the big scheme

of things nor does it stop such occurrences from happening. However, I personally believe that one should keep an open mind and perhaps, even entertain some occult ideaologies.....???? Well, there it is, the first time ever put down in writing! Hope you've enjoyed reading about my personal experience and "Thank You" for reading.

Remember this: "Not all that is, is seen"

10-26-19 By: Dex McLaughlin ©
© Copyright 2019

My plan was to fill this book, it didn't work that way but most are legible and if not let to work together and get this done.

Thanks.

Dex

– UNTITLED –

Ignorance echoes - as does a thunder rumble,
    hearts grow cold

Cannot mute these sounds, struggling to be humble.

Headgames, is this the way of mankind
    Dog eat dog

Only the weak will be left behind.

So it is that the strong shall survive
    Deep dark earth
In reality - dead - not really alive.

Love is acquired, hatred istilled in the heart
    emotion in the shadows
In fear of being torn apart.

Past long gone, freedom took for granted
    lonely existence

Meaningless memories left to be enchanted.

Love is weak - hatred so contagious
    Fear not the haters

Rise above opposition and be courageous.

Topics:			
X-mas *17	Halloween *13	Thanksgiving 57	B-days *25
• • •	• •		
Love *37	Hate *21	Govt. 53	Seasons 65
	•		
Recovery *33	Inspirational *29	Family *41	Spirituality 61
		• •	
Success 45	Failure *41	Malice 49	Health 69

- RECOVERY - UNTITLED

Recovery to me may not be what it is to you,
    piercing the flames
as the souls that do make it one very few.

Hitting rock bottom so deep for so long,
    Hindsight's 20-20
oh the many things been done so wrong.

Having the coverage to admit your defeat
    if in denial
The pain of history will surely repeat.

Refuse to let addiction, cause your demise,
    for the non-believer's -
a million dollars later, look, its me, surprise!

Honestly though, lets keep things real
    nearing numbness
to the point where its unhealthy not to feel.

When the rain seems to thick for you to move forward
    at least look through it
to the goal that you must push toward.

- MUDSLIDE -

What's it like to feel again ??? I can't remember

Was there ever such a time when the moon influenced the tide,
     When the stars shined
and the rain caused destruction by way of - "mudslide!"

Feeling content in your self made hell,
     ever so vulnerable
as Satan rings his wicked bell!

I went out, I went off, I can't stand the fuckin ride
     unsacred so it consumes me
in this twisted ???carnage they call - mudslide!

Mass confusion of the future-uncaring of the past
     what would be the point
in finding happiness that is sure to never last

Evil penetrates this very depths of our souls,
     if you're in denial
open your eyes and take a hard look at the youth in our schools

Seems to me they went out they can't stand this fucking ride,
     unclean souls try to teach them
in this twisted carnage they call - mudslide!

Never-mind the ???present, who cares about society
     what is it truly
that you were to make your #1 priority

Hatred in the heart - hatred in their stares
     what is peace
in a world be full of ???greed where no-one really cares

So we say this ain't so bad - I kinda like this side
     come with me my friend
though this twisted carnage I come to know as - mudslide!

You want in - you want out make up your fuckin mind
     The ship of souls is leaving
this hatred and carnage and the sickness of mankind.

Dex - 6-23-05
"From the "Darkside"

- MUDSLIDE -
???

Was there ever such a time when the moon influenced the tide,
     When the stars shined
and the rain caused destruction by way of - "mudslide!"

Feeling content in your self made hell,
     ever so vulnerable
as Satan rings his wicked bell!

I want out, I want off, I can't stand this fucking ride,
     unsacred sail consumes me
in this twisted carnage they call - 'Mudslide!"

Mass confusion of the future - uncaring of the past,
     what would be the point
in finding happiness that is sure to "never" last!

Evil penetrates, the very depths of our souls,
     if your in denial
open your eyes and take a hard look at the youth in our schools!

Seems to me they want out they can't stand this fucking ride,
     unclean souls try to teach them
in this twisted carnage they call - "Mudslide!"

Never mind the present, who cares about society,
     what is it truly
that you wish to make your number one priority!

Hatred in their hearts - hatred in their stares,
     what is peace
in a world so full of greed where no-one really cares!

So we say this ain't so bad - I kinda like this ride,
     come with me my friend
through this twisted carnage I come to know as - "Mudslide!"

You want in - you want out - make up your fucking mind,
     the ship of souls is leaving
this hatred and carnage caused by the sickness in mankind!

Dex - 6-23-05

MALICE
- INSANE PAIN -

Once again trapped within, can't perceive or believe. Searching for an escape,
    can't seem to find one, no matter how hard I try
Darkness invades my light - this madness must die.

Stealing your pleasure from my pain, just what is it that you hope to gain?
Drawing on my weakness to fuel your fire, only to fall victim of your own desires.
Behave what you will, I am content with my pain, for it was my pleasure that drove me insane!

Web of corruption - self absorbed seduction - headed for destructions
No use in complaining there's nothing to be gaining - sky is always raining
unable from sustaining this insane pain!

Lost in a fantasy, desperate to rationalize this wicked behavior, paradoxical defeat fool, there is no savior!
This thing I see looking back at me, so abstract, ignorant in fact, what has become of me?
The sun bleeds red, another soul dead, what's left to be said? When there's no one left to blame,

the truth be known, nothing will ever be the same. Always in the wrong lane, chasin down the weakest
train - so sick insane when I feel this pain - can't seem to put a face to my name.
Web of corruption - self absorbed seduction - headed for destruction

No use complaining there's nothing to be gaining - sky is always raining
unable from sustaining this insane pain!

727- 424- 4985

HATE
- Untitled -

Stupid people - there seems to be a ripple effect,
    an ignorance highway
of idiots who deserve none but demand your respect.

So full of themselves that its truly quite pathetic,
    un-original people
incapable of being real - let alone authentic.

thriving on your misery so that they don't feel alone,
    blood suckers -
if yo let them they'll drain you by right to the bone.

Stay unaffected by these true-born lasers,
    be true to yourself
there's nothing to be gained from these integrity abusers.

- UNTITLED -

Why oh why should I even try
Liquid skies from the tears that flood my eyes
I will not front to try and disguise

All the years I've tried - blood, sweat, and lies
You know its bad when the angel cries
No comfort in any amount of highs

So why oh why must I even try
I just wanna go where the angel flies
Refrain from this pain - grant me my demise

This request shouldn't come as a total surprise
You've tortured me with every tool you could devise
But the joke's on you - no longer will I improvise

Sleep for you shall be eternity - try that on for size
Quite modest in comparison there's nothin left to compromise.

B-DAY (3)

Inspirational
- Untitled -

Depression is nothing lust a selfish state of mind,
    woe is me
get over it - yeah sometimes life is cruel and unkind.

There's always someone else worse off than what you are,
    suffering is non-stop
Wounds do heal, give it time, you'll learn to live with the scar

Sometimes it helps to write down what you feel,
    exposing your weakness
integrates into perspective, to yourself, keep things real.

Set your mind to success and focus on that goal,
    conqueor those demons
don't be stuck on stupid and be left the laughing fool,

Be not blinded by the false reality that nobody cares,
    its comforting to know
that the ultimate love awaits you atop those heavenly stains.

RECOVERY (1)

LOVE
- Decades Memories -

Thoughts of past relationships occasionally cross your mind
    its a natural process
to wonder whether they're happy or fell victim to the unkind.

the past will be the past. Theres nothing you can do
    entertaining the thought
that if you think of them, they must surely think of you.

A song triggers a memory of days, long gone
    Decade has passed - &
you cherish those precious years for its been so long

the beauty of it all is the memories that we create
    but one they solid
Rather than ones that cause nothing but grief and heartache.

Your memories provide a sense of who you are today,
    ponder that thought
for who would you be if circumstance were to strip your memory away.

© Copyright 2021
Dex McLaughlin

FAILURE (1)

Success (1)

Malice
- Untitled -

???gh this morning fog I cannot see
    unforseen danger
??? end of life is near - my fate to be

Total darkness, what did I miss
    is this purgatory
??? or am I forever lost in Satans abyss

No, this cannot be - for I was forgivin,
    fantasy friend
for you are now among the un-livin

The irony of it all is at times I wished I would die,
    frightened beyond belief
never again will I enjoy the sunny blue sky.

Death equals the sum of all fears
    my legacy untold
as my memory fades into the yester-years.

GOVT. (1)

THANKSGIVING (1)

SPIRITUALITY (1)

Seasons (1)

- A Statement -

We are one in all, come my demise, stumble, or fall emotionally fueled by the flames burning deep within our hearts

Hindered spirits clinging to hope, that the dirt we carry will forever remain filtered through out the determination to never again answer death and despairs wicked call.

The human race as a whole seems to be troubled by the darker side of many of modern religions, giving in to our greedy self conscience alter - ego - begging forgiveness from a non existent entity, repeatedly falling victim to ourselves - our own worse enemy.

This one I personally wrote to my own mom and thought it would be a nice touch for the book don't ya think

Dex

2-2-21

Mom,

Hey, how are you? I hope good! I just thought I'd drop you a few lines in hopes that I may brighten up your day, and lift your spirit ??? ... Being as though I'm always asking for something or another......Not the case here.....I want you to know mom, that you are a "wonderful" person, and I love you with all my heart! Know that everything you've done for me, and still do, is deeply "appreciated!" Not only are you a wonderful mother, you are an "awesome" friend as well!☒ Know that I do have a "conscience", and a warm heart,...I "sincerely" regret the times that I've lied to you, hurt your feelings, stole from you, or made you cry. You did not deserve those things from me.! "Please" take "comfort" in knowing that, that was not the "real" me, and that I am truly sorry mom! ??? You are a kind hearted human-being by nature, and people should feel "privileged", and, "thankful", to have you on their side. I know I do! Also, know that I will not "forsake" you in your time of need....That I will be there for you in any way that I can, just as you have been there for me! You did the best you could at raising us, I have the utmost respect for you mom - and you should feel no guilt! So mom, this letter isn't to ask you for anything, or for you to do anything...its simply meant to bring a warm smile to your face, and touch your heart... to help make you feel that you are truly "appreciated" by me! So if, and when you feel any sadness, read these words of love, and may they bring you joy!! I'll close now by saying, please keep me in your prayers, as you are always in mine. And may peace and contentment be with you in your heart always, & forever! And last, but not least..."I love you mom!"

P.S. HAVE A WONDERFUL DAY!!

Love,
Dex

© Copyright 2017
Dexter McLaughlin

THE STORY OF AN EXPERIENCE

2-2-21
Dexter

Time: Who knows?!   Mon. 2-13-12   Place: Houtzdale R.H.V. Isolation

It seems as though I'm in a trance - a victim of my own circumstance. There's nothin for me to feel right now but numb? I feel so helpless. I am at the mercy of a corrupt legal system! And a diabolical department of corrections, or rather, dept. of "corruptions," to put it more truer!

I have alot of positive going for me and things could definitely could be worse, but damn do I seem to be living my own curse. Its as if the legal system is a mighty dragon out to devour me, with its powerful jaws of scrutiny, evil eyes of media propaganda, and let me not forget the shattered lives, and broken spirt(s), and a smoke filled forever tainted past that the fire only from the belly of the beast his-self can create! It's as though that beast wants to define who I am, but I know that it can only do it through public opinion - for no beast such as a legal system, can truly define who one is. I knew I'm not that person they make me to be I'm a kind hearted soul, eager to give, share; love, to be loved, I have an awesome relationship to offer - I know that - but do you? The reader of these words? Do you believe in the words you read or hear in the media, all the hyped up drama, that sadly, human nature tends to strive on. Do you feed on the brutal attacks of peoples character? Or would you believe in and of the words of a poor lonely soul like mine? I wanna share my love with a woman of kindred spirit, and it just seems as though that day will never get here.

So here I am, faced with yet another consequence of my past; the Law of "Cause & Effect" dictates that, whatsoever a man soweth, that he shall also reap. My past is have to haunt me? I cannot begin to even describe what my poor spirit has felt these last 10 years, especially these past 72 hours and counting unless one experiences the horrible trauma first hand, no amount of words can paint the picture of a past so filled with negative vibrations. These feelings, are a mixture of, hurt, anger, betrayed confusion, lonliness, bewilderment, lost, scared resentment, exhaustion, and a few select more, can you imagine putting these feelings into a blender and mixing them up?! What kind of emotional being would such a concauction render??? Most likely a negative and unhealthy one don't ya think?...Which leads me to the strong side of my spirit - strong only because of the troubled of past and of which I write to you now, has helped to cultivate. It is not easy always finding strength, but I must find it, and "surely" I'm drawing it from some reservoir of power - a guide glimpse into my soul should reveal that power: I take great comfort in knowing that one day, I will be sitting check to check with the love of my life. Somewhere, on a warm summer night, under a full moon, just staring at the stars listening to music of the crickets, carrying their melody through the midnite breeze, just simply enjoying each others presence. Not caring about anything else at that moment. If one should open their eyes a bit more, perhaps you even had a glimpse into your own soul?

However, that thought totally relaxes me, for I know in my heart that it will truly happen, why are you so sure you might ask? Because as strongly as I yearn for and desire a kindred spirit, I am sure to draw a similar kind my way, the laws of attraction through animal magnetism coupled with strong course/thought/desire wave energy. I'm sure to attract an alike spirit, all I truly feel right now at present is just plain numb what can I truly do? Hope for the best is definitley a given. I'm already a year into a 6 month sentence? And still not paroled on current sentence. And my whole routine has been turned upside down. I'm stripped of all my personal belongings, slapped with brand new changes and thrown into a isolation cell with hardly the bare necessities around a bunch of animal wanna-be gangsta retards! I'm just like, "really?", I keep thinkin of that day I spoke of. And believe me, I will cherish that moment when it happens. I do take alot of comfort and draw some strength from a certain female whom surely she knows. That energy that drew her to write me may be responsible for the best happiness we've ever known? That story is yet to be realized. However, I feel so blessed that she chose to write me for I truly know that she is sincere. And that mean the world to me. She seems like an awesome woman and I'm really excited about our friendship! If more comes of it, it shall come of its own accord, the natural flow of things is my best chance at true love.

So again, the only way to describe how I feel right now is "numb" - to me, money is the root of all "corruption", and the love & desire for that money is the root of all "evil", is this not so? Money equals power, so so sad, but so true! Money for me right now would definitley merit me some peace of mind and a somewhat calm state of being, cause I would atleast be able to obtain a lawyer, whom could handle the legal litigations that I am ignorant of and unable to handle correctly or wisely myself love to corrupt conditions beyond my control! Atleast be able to wound that wicked dragon, for slaying it is impossible...If you only truly knew what my poor soul has this far endured, you would most certainly understand my present feelings, would you not??

There is no worse feeling in the world than that of utter and complete lonliness! Never take kindness, compassion, love, and genuine concern for granted! For it is a double edged sword! Those are real states of being, and it is real heartache and happiness they produce - you will feel the effects from whatever cause it is that you sent in motion; I must add to the lonliness, I won't mention the unconditional love that one feels from a mother, in my case, she has saved me from the total complete feeling of being alone, she has been there for me through it all. And for that I am truly grateful! For I know that same folks do not even have that! I truly feel for them & send my best blessings - I do have a heart, and oh so much love to give.

They say that misery loves company "And how true it is! How "selfish" it is of us to want someone else to feel the pain and misery we are feeling! Or take comfort in knowing that they're worse off than us, how sick is that type of thinking!? I mean truly? Its utter madness! But yet it is a true fact of human nature, that no-one can deny! Sure, there are those of us out there that do not feel in this way, but we are exceptions to the rule, for we had to cultivate and condition our inner-being before we were ever able to express a genuine compassion for another soul!!

In summary of this enormous thought, I must admit that it is this spiritual side of my nature that is puling me through this. I keep picturing my happy thought of the love of my life, hand in hand living happily in our own piece of paradise. Happy and content with each other, with ourselves, spiritually, emotionally, mentally, physically & financially. And truly living life in tune with the vibrations of our spirits, and that of mother nature. What the hell is so wrong with wanting that!!?? I say nothing! Which is why I will have it!! All I can say at this point in time, is that I truly know, that I am a star she waiting to shine in anything I do. For it is people who learn life's lesson the hard way that shine the brightest!! The best advice I can give to myself is love one another, be true to thy own self. And lead by example, for it is only through our actions do our words become truth, and change becomes manifest. "Dex 2-13-12"

Dexter McLaughlin

This I wrote for my son to see, which he hasn't yet!

He was only 6 or 7 when I wrote this, I would love for him to read this in my book!

- MY LEGACY -

When I'm dead and gone I would want my son and family, even my friends and acquaintances to be inspired by my determination and willingness to overcome the many obstacles that I faced in life. I would want them to feel it in their hearts and truly see how much I've matured into a responsible caring father who knew of his shortcomings but yet had the courage in hindsight to learn from his mistakes, a man who overcame his demons and persevered into the future without letting past failures weigh him down.

I would want them to recognize that I was driven by love and had a determination to succeed in life, realizing that my past failures had only made me a stronger man. I would have wanted to blow their skepticism so far out of sight that I secured a spot in their hearts forever.

Josh would say to himself and others with a proud sparkle in his eye, my dad was a great man because he took control of his life and accepted responsibility and became the father to me that he never had. He showed me that you can make your dreams come true, because he accomplished everything that he set out to do. He gave me direction in my life and paved the way for me to become a strong productive individual. He did the things necessary to ensure that I didn't make the same mistakes he did. He showed me that life is what you make it, and that you can turn a troubled past into a wonderful future, which he did whole-heartedly. And I love him very much for that. Because of my dad, I am a very successful, and responsible married man with two beautiful children of my own.

My father took his past and used it as a stepping stone to give me my values and the integrity in life to provide for my children and family, as he did for me and his family. He made it possible for me to break the cycle, had he not had the courage and willingness to become a responsible father, my family values and dignity wouldn't be what they are today, and history would have been destined to repeat itself. And for that, his grandchildren will grow up knowing that their grandfather was a well loved and respected man. He was very inspirational and touched the hearts of everyone who knew him. The day he died was a very sad day for all of us.

It's been 20 years since his passing, and my feelings towards him are as strong today as they were then! I truly hope to have an impact on my childrens lives in such a way as my dad did mine, so that they too will be left with precious memories. So that they will show the love and affection to their children that my dad so passionately showed me. My father is my hereo, and I will be forever grateful of his ability to bring the positive out of the negative.

"Penny, I want to thank you for your kindness and willingness to share your knowledge of a parent with me, and I'm sure I speak for most of the class also. Just know that you have been a positive inspiration to me as a father and that a child will benefit as a result of your efforts. In the future, I'm sure that I will reflect back upon your class. Thank you so much!"

I (I could ??? an infinity of roses, ???)

So you ??? will know my loyalty the way that is should ???
Anything ???

33 years of beauty is this dream or is this real
This love is my ??? for you to feel

1   Just a quick thinking of you poem so that it may brighten up your day, keep me close to your heart and I promise you girl it'll be OK.

2   No need to feel alone our hopes and dreams are not lost, your happiness is not measure in which I will never count the cost.

3   33 years of beauty this ain't a dream I'm so glad you are real, and undying love floods my heart that I so long for you to feel.

4   If I could send you an infinity of roses I so eagerly would so- your soul may know my loyalty the way I feel that it should.

5   Let this year be the beginning of a never ending ride, forgetting the pains of the past forever standing by each others side.

6   I'm forever under your spell as you turn my grey skies blue perhaps there may come a day when I can say, that I love you? ???

"MIDNITE BREEZE"

Midnite breeze of love.

Is pulling us so near.

Just the fragrance of your scent.

Rids me of my fear.

Surrounded by hate.

In a world so full of greed.

Comforting thoughts of you.

Are all I'll ever need.

Seconds turn to minutes.

Those minutes into hours.

Making our sweet love.

Upon a bed of flowers.

The sky so blue above us.

The ground so green below.

You're always on my mind Michele.

That you need to know.

The rose of love shall bloom.

In due time my sweet.

Blossoming like magic.

Until the day we meet.

Once that rose has blossomed.

We shall never part our ways.

I will always love you dearly.

Until the end of days.

Midnite breeze of sorrows.

Worry not my love.

We shall ride these waves together.

Underneath the stars above.

Should a star come shooting.

Into the midnite sea.

Holding you forever.

Is what my wish would be.

DESTINY

A spirit like mine is surely destined for more,
I must be cautious on the wicked and evil allure.
These horrible feelings are an un-necessary grief,
The joys of love and honesty are anything but brief.

Everything I'm experiencing is a self made hell,
Falling prey to some unseen malicious and evil spell.
I've cheated myself out of so much in life,
Blood from these wounds drip like water from the blade of a painful knife.

Oh how my heart feels so bitter and sore,
A balance in mind, body, and soul necessary to even out the score.
Perhaps one day in this journey I will meet my true soulmate,
Is it written in my stars or is it simply just fate?

We are here but briefly and then suddenly gone,
To face the music of our angel's song.
Will it be darkness or shall I be made to see,
We're creating our own heaven & hell in choosing our destiny.

Dex © Copyright 2012
3/13/12

- UNTITLED -

The sun rises in the east and at dawn the sparrow sings,
Life is always changing, that's just the nature of things.
In reviewing our past we can plainly see...
The person we were twenty years ago - today, simply cannot be.

We are forever living with in a constant state of change,
To ignore this reality hinders our potential out of focus range.
For we never truly walk through the same stream twice,
Coming to know our eternal soul involves necessary sacrifice.

When this is realized our disappointments will slowly cease,
Only then will peace and enlightenment forever increase.
Become not ignorant to the law of cause and effect,
Our actions throw us in the poll of consequence, in which we become the elect!

We must never become a prisoner of our mind,
For it is only a tool for the soul and is often unkind.
Always thrive for goodness and be pure at heart,
And know...that in awakening our conscience - we must "wisely" do our part.

Dex 1-7-12
© Copyright 2012

- SEMBLANCE -

I think of you and my heart beats out a rhyme,
　　　　spelling out true words of love
　　until the end of time.

Longing for companionship & love forever more,
　　　　happiness a treasure
　　a key that unlocks the door.

Within your eyes a beauty that is far and few,
　　　　you spanked a flame yeah your to blame
　　For setting my heart anew.

Coming upon the future the years are passing by,
　　　　mending sacred heartaches
　　your eyes forever dry.

No matter how insidious this life it seems to be,
　　　　past, present, and future
　　you are the only one for me.

Put these thoughts together and hopefully you will feel,
　　　　the magic in our love
　　and know that it's for real.

It is said that whatsoever a man soweth

That to he shall also reap,

No amount of words could paint a picture

Of the misery that I still keep.

Alone I am forced to face the consequences

Reality has settled in,

Broken dreams, shattered pasts

Defines this beast within.

Who is this self destructive demon

That only I could have created?

Steadily walking this twisted path

Realizing the whole time,

I'm the one holdin the line

To its deceitful deadly wrath.

This battlefield in my soul keeps me playin the fool

And it seems the beast may win,

But I'm holdin strong

Just don't know how long,

Oh how I cannot give in.

I reach out at length

But find I'm lacking in strength

To grasp this peace and happiness that I desire,

So much love in my heart

I'm so eager to start,

Rekindling my passions long lost fire.

Such a painful shame

When people seem lame

For it truly plays tricks on the mind,

When you've only found love

When push came to shove,

And you still feel left behind.

Its best to be safe than sorry

This is what they say,

Loves not just some game and

I'm not to blame,

Forgive me but

I choose not to play.

I've opened my heart

Only to be torn apart

All I ask is for a love that will last,

I wanna be sure my

Cause my heart is still sore,

From the not so distant past.
Another misconception turned
Into a lifes lesson.
I shall move forward
And will overcome,
Through the grains of sand,
I'm playing lifes hand,
Never forgetting where it is
That I truly come from.
The truth by far
Is your only true start - Oh but
How much stranger it is than fiction,
So wrong all the while
Stepping down from denial, facing
Adversary with much more conviction.
So I've taken some falls
Yeah time changes all
I can still feel so much pain,
But I'm steadily soaring higher
As my spirit grows wiser,
For I know there is much more to gain.
Flesh turns to bones
And ashes to dust,
[When friends become strangers]
Who can you trust?
Time does not heal
It only numbs what you feel and
Opens your eyes to the truth.

This poem is for you
In its own unique style
I pray it warms your heart
And that it makes you smile.
Fourty four years of beauty
May you be blessed forever
You are a timeless treasure
And I shall forsake you never.
Growing old is a privilege
And is not a right
Forever enduring lifes struggles
Always fighting the good fight.
I am ever so grateful
That not all hope is lost
For nothing that is great
Ever comes without a cost.
So lost in your love
Baby please don't you cry
Our souls shall take flight
To where the angels fly.
May you let sweet love
Be stronger than false pride
I shall remain true and faithful
And forever will I stand - by your side!

- DECADES MEMORY -

Thoughts of past relationships occasionally cross your mind,
    it's a natural process
To wonder whether they're happy or fell victim to the unkind.

The past is the past there's nothing we can do,
    entertaining the thought
that if you think of them - they must surely think of you.

A song triggers a memory for its been so long,
    the future consumes the present
As you cherish the thoughts of days long gone.

Products of the past are the memories that we create,
    Make them worthwhile
full of love and honor instead of greed and hate.

So it is that your memory provides a sense of who you are today,
    Ponder that thought
For who would you be if circumstance were to strip your memory away?!

SOUL FIRES

Peace of mind is where we need to be,
    utilizing our powers
as madness and chaos profoundly surround thee.
Near non existent in a world full of hate,
    wondering about aimlessly
desperate to foresee one's own fate.
Ambitions running high ??? and low,
    as the fiends await
the time for our youth the power to bestow.
Fires burning within the soul,
    sinful desires in purgatory
thereby forsaking the golden rule!
Inspiration coming from destination unknown,
    as the seeds of our destiny
are unknowingly being sewn!
The sun goes down and the moon will rise
    so shall the master of deception
eagerly corrupting the mind with tantalizing evil cries.
Defying lifes woes as we battle this corruption,
    with pride locked tight inside
we await our masters sovereign abruption.
Heed to these words as there is evil for hire,
where shall you bewhen judgment is upon your soulfire desire?!

My life right now one big mess,

I brought it upon myself - this I confess.

But I still must face each dying hour,

with regrets from the past that I cannot devour.

Just when you thought you had it all,

Satans wrath comes down and lets you take that fall.

My minds in a blurr as I face the unknown,

curious of the future and of what seeds need to be sewn.

My spirits are low and my body is weak,

Serenity and peace of mind is what I ultimately seek.

Had I found Jesus earlier in my life,

my heart wouldn't be bleeding like it's been stuck with a knife.

He who reads this - their world falling apart,

take heed to these words for they truly come from the heart!

Mark 13:5-23   Luke 16:19-31 "Dex 2000"

Deuteronomy 32:35

Matthew 11:28

Romans 12

DESTINY
???

A spirit like mine is surely destined for more,

I must be cautious on the wicked and evil allure.

These horrible feelings are an un-necessary grief,

The joys of love and honesty are anything but brief.

Everything I'm experiencing is a self made hell,

Falling prey to some unseen malicious and evil spell.

I've cheated myself out of so much in life,

Blood from these wounds drip like water from the blade of a painful knife.

Oh how my heart feels so bitter and sore,

A balance in mind, body, and soul necessary to even out the score.

Perhaps one day in this journey I will meet my true soulmate,

Is it written in my stars or is it simply just fate?

We are here but briefly and then suddenly gone,

To face the music of our angel's song.

Will it be darkness or shall I be made to see,

We're creating our own heaven & hell in choosing our destiny.

Dex © Copyright 2012

3/13/12

???

VISIONS

Lonliness is a feeling that seems to have no remorse,
    I pray just for today
giving thanks and letting his will run its course.

Somedays I feel deserted and on my own,
    at times unable to realize
that there is one who truly cares and that I am not alone.

Sitting and watching the world pass by,
    curious of the future
and seeking the strength to keep my head held high.

Wanting to be loved and also to love,
    sometimes selfish of the fact
that there is great power beyond the blue sky above.

In my heart I know that God will prevail,
    as he builds his ship of soldiers
I await his return and know that I am ready to sail.

Just remember you have to take the bad with the good,
    giving thanks for another day
For he may take away tomorrow - as you know that he could.

???

Dex McLaughlin
2000 © Copyright

"TIME"

Time is what we call a curious thing,
    for thou shall not know
just what time will bring.

It may bring us pleasure it may bring us pain,
    it might make us question our sanity
or drive us completely insane.

Time may go slow it may go fast,
    for the second hand keeps ticking
as we create our own past.

We take if one day at a time we don't give it much thought,
    we are selfish of the things
that we so desperately sought.

One thing we must know in this day and age,
    is that the time will come
when we must turn the page.

The future may be bright - if may be glowing,
    for what that next page brings
we have no way of knowing.

We need not know what song the future might chime,
    for that of which destiny
will always take time!

???

1994

- EXALT - (TRINITY DENIED)

Judge me not those of the right handed path,
> for it is you
who will suffer in the coming wrath!!

"Do what thou will shall be
The whole of the law"

Uncertainty haunts my thoughts - The present fades into the past,
> the bells of doom are pending
into the darkness I shall cast.

Satan is king do you not see through your shameful eyes,
> fear not for your souls
From the abyss he will rise.

Indecision determines our fate,
> clouds of despair
to those who are governed by hate.

Do not be hindered by the unfortunate weak,
> wandering aimlessly
For they know not what they seek.

Living life proud and guilt free,
> retribution to the church
Forever will it be in misery.

Sin is bad in the eyes of our God,
> we the pagan legion
smash through your walls of fraud.

To a religion that condemns me for all I enjoy
> to the foe
will I forever annoy.

Imposing your will where it is most unwanted,
> free-thinkers unite
walking among you protected and undaunted.

Congregation, is that not a form of a "cult",
> waging war on yourself
evil accused though it is you at fault.

Evil laughs in the face of the hypocrite,
  may the flames pierce your soul
For my diamond sparkles in your hell-fire pit.

Lucifer never fell to the earth, Lucifer is really God; refer to Yahweh by the name of Adonay; Yaheh The God of Evil because he forces man to be subservient to his repressive dictates.

  Masons have their own Luciferian calendar, where Christians our based on the years before (B.C.) and after (A.D.) the birth of Christ, Masons count its your with the suffix A.L. means Anno Lucis or "Year of light" (Lucifer).

TRINITY DENIED

Genesis 3:4-5
John 9-11

7-7-07

TRINITY DENIED

???

Dex McLaughlin © Copyright

Freemasonry has a plan of salvation which is based on invitation of their savior, Hiram Abiff - who lost the secret name of God while he was building the great pyramid, as punishment he was entombed alive in the pyramid, salvation refers to being brought from the material to the spiritual; i.e. when man returns to his "forgotten inherent spirituality", the degree of the master mason is symbolical of old age which allows a person to happily reflect on a well spent life and to "die of a glorious immortality". Salvation is a step-by-step process enlightenment, which comes through the masonic degrees and their mysteries the "Angel of the Abyss - The chief demon whose name is "Abaddon Revelation chpt.

Revelation 16:14 9;

- INSPIRE -

Intimate memories, so many we will make,
    for I know
sincere true love sh**a**ll never forsake.

Living each day as it were our last together,
    this madness succumbs
marching hand in hand through lifes stormy weather.

Open wings gracing the blue skies,
    your beauty I see
glistening so bright through your angel eyes.

Venus is ours not a soul to be found,
    spinning in harmony
to the beating of our hearts sweet pulsating sound.

Erotica between us nothing can compare,
    forever in eternity
to the ending of days with no other I'd share.

Yearning to rid you of life's miserable woes,
    any such chance
to give you new life as that of a blossoming rose.

On through the night into the witching hour,
    in unison we chant
for the ailment within you will be forever devoured.

Unstoppable power comes from deep within,
    together forever
in this battle we will win!

Dex 7-16-07
© Copyright 2007

- OMINOUS -

So full of love yet dominated by hate,
     emptiness fills the void
For the tides of despair do not discriminate.

Broken promises of a better tomorrow,
     mature into ugly
shattered dreams amid true sorrow.

Longing for a purpose unable to break the curse,
     chains of mayhem torture
the unforgiving pain grows maliciously worse.

Darkness thereafter, farewell to the dying saint,
     the inevitable has befallen
chrome wheels of death so infinite underneath polished paint.

Happiness held captive threatening to break free,
     windows to the soul
closing with silent relief for all eternity.

This afterlife I chose so peaceful and sene,
     many souls are roaming
for the truth I have seen.

Dex 7-16-07
® Copyright 07

- INFERNAL FLAME -

Just a quick thinking of you poem so that it may brighten up your day,
Keep me close to your heart and I promise you girl it'll be OK.
No need to feel alone our hopes and dreams are not lost,
Your happiness is my pleasure in which I will never count the cost.

Many years of beauty this ain't a dream I'm so glad that you are real,
An undying love floods my heart that I so long for you to feel.
If I could send you an infinity of roses I'd most gratefully would,
So that your soul may know my loyalty the way I feel that it should.

Let this year be the beginning of a never ending ride,
Forgetting the pains of the past forever standing by each others side.
I'm forever under your spell as you turn my grey skies blue,
Perhaps there may come a day when I can say, that I love you?

- SEASONAL BLISS -

Snowflakes mingle with cold November rain,
    influencing our thoughts
With the joys of happiness we've yet too acclaim.

Season of love once again draws near,
    diminishing the sorrows
Of another passing year.

Tis the eve of anticipation under a warning moon,
    children unwittingly prolong their intent
For the first hint of daylight cannot arrive a moment to soon.

Christmas has arrived under the glow of a bright morning star,
    anticipation turns to excitement
Priceless are the sounds of joy being heard by the heaven and afar.

Thirteen lunar cycles set forth in wake of each passing year,
    only through love
Shall we overcome and conquer our fears.

Dex McLaughlin
© Copyright 11-16-07

- UNTITLED -

Within the darkest recess of the mind
Invoke the force thy soul to bind.
Eyes wide shut ignorance so blind
Stimulate the senses and power you'll find.

Mental martial artist the spirit runs free
Eyes wide open but you still don't see.
Monitoring thoughts to never lose sight
Wisdom is the key unlocking the mystery of night.

The self will always win right out
In the game of morality someone else wins the bout.
Attention being given to thoughts dwelled on today
For they will surely manifest in the future some way.

Attempting not to be an all souls friend
For this is foolishness and meets a dead end.
Wealthful of knowledge amounts to stagnation
It means absolutely nothing without application.

There's a right way to look at things and a right way to live
Death has no mercy and does not forgive.
Outcomes in this life are not ruled by fate
Realize this reality before it's to late.

Dex M
S.C.I Rockview
1-21-09
© Copyright 2009

"Epigram"

As I walk and look into the darkness of the night,
    I see cold November raindrops
glisten through the prison yard light.

My heart turns bitter as I await this nightmare to end,
    only to walk that lonely road -
to no-where with me my only friend.

No-one really knows what I truly feel inside,
    ignorant to the fact
that some must endure this twisted and evil ride.

Nothing has ever been truly what they seemed,
    creating a world of mistakes
Blind to the reality - they may never be redeemed.

Walking in madness as a result of my past,
    eager to escape this darkness
of an underlying evil that is sure to last.

Realizing that hopes and dreams are still within my grip
    crashing through waves of sorrow
with a bitter vengeance such as that of a battleship

2-2-21
© Copyright 2021
Dexter McLaughlin

"SHADOW WINGS" BY: DEX MCLAUGHLIN

Dancing in the shadows of butterflies on into the night,
    falling in love again -,
Under a sheet of stars in the pale moon light.

The divine angels share their love with only but a few,
    sacred as the universe -
All the sunsets on the oceans have nothing on you.

You are the spark that ignites my fire,
    the very essence of your soul -
Majestically fuels the flames of desire.

As I breathe in your beauty I can taste your love,
    Blessed with your loyal devotion -
through it all especially when push comes to shove.

The moon casts a spell as an angel sings,
    the cadence of heartache -
Fading away upon the precious love of butterfly wings.

Soaring to the boat of our own wings high above the stars,
    gracefully gliding towards -
the divine love for eternity that is rightfully ours!

Dex 2019

Drafted on 3-2-19 for my baby, Judy Miller/Judy McLaughlin,"

© Copyright 2019

"Food For Thought"

"If we are lucky enough to find our complimentary soul, the divine steps in to create a third entity - a spirit companion - whose only job is too watch over the two us (you) (us). But if you turn your back on your beloved, if you "consciously" turn away from your beloved, the one designed to love your human heart into perfection - then the spirit companion leaves you it "never" returns. And the goodness that was meant to be will never come to pass!" ???

Dex © Copyright 2021

???

"EUOLOGY"

Hey Babe, here's my latest poem:
(gonna get that book published sooner or labrē)
- Eulogy - by: Dex McLaughlin © Copyright 2019

For those who have passed, I wish you the best,
    for the time has come
For you to finally rest.

May you find peace within your heavenly gate,
    finally knowing the secret
As to whether our destinies are governed by fate?

Each departed soul I love in my own special way,
    finding solace in the fact
That we shall meet again some other day.

We should pray for our departed in sheer thanksgiving,
    as they rise above the stars
To become our guardian angels among the living.

As for us whom are left behind,
    be true to thy own self
And peace in the end you shall find.

"Nope you liked it sweetness ???
    add it to my collection"

"I Love You"

- SOUL FIRES -

Peace of mind is where we need to be,
        utilizing our powers
as madness and chaos profoundly surround thee.

Near non existent in a world full of hate,
        wandering about aimlessly
desperate to foresee one's own fate.

Ambitions running high and low,
        as the fiends await
the time for our youth the power to bestow.

Fires burning within the soul,
        sinful thoughts in purgatory
thereby forsaking the golden rule.

Inspiration coming from destination unknown,
        as the seeds of our future
are unknowingly being sewn.

The sun goes down and the moon will rise,
        so shall the master of deception
eagerly corrupting the mind with tantalizing evil cries.

Defying life's woes as we battle this corruption,
        with pride locked tight inside
we await our masters sovereign abruption.

Heed to these words as there is evil for hire,
        where shall you be
when judgement is upon your soulfire desire?

- Hell Can't Stop My Love -

I do believe that God above

He created you for me to love

He picked you from all the rest

Because He know I'd love you best

I once had a heart so true

My love for you is oh so true

I long for the joy to be with you

Forever shedding the heartless that sever

You and me babe - soulmates forever!

And if I should die before you do

Be at heavens gate searching for you

If you don't show on that fateful day

Then I'll know you've gone the other way

I'll give away my angel wings

My golden harp and other things

You'll know my love is so strong and true

that I'd come down to hell just to be with you.

I'm gonna tongue punch
<u>yer man</u> in her fart box.

Printed in the United States
by Baker & Taylor Publisher Services